TABLE OF CONTENTS

CREDITS

Bábá Náma Kevalam: Shrii Shrii Anandamurti
Music, Song Lyrics (except Tiny Green Island): Jyoshna La Trobe
Editor: Erik Azzopardi
Design: Kavita Neumannova
Layout: Jano Stefanik
Photos: Didi Ananda Prama, Jyoshna La Trobe, Sanjayo Kumar Mahato, Karun Towsey
Published by: Croi publishing, Co.Clare, Ireland
www.croipublishing.com

FOREWORD

I have been on the kirtan and meditation path of Ananda Marga since 1975. Being a musician already when I began meditation, I found kiirtan somewhat daunting with so many people singing and dancing, some in tune, some not, some in rhythm, some not. The fact that it was inclusive of everyone was very inspiring yet there were challenges for me musically. However, these challenges quickly gave way to a deep inner purpose as a musician and a devotee: to compose kiirtan that is sincerely felt, musically 'sound', and also works collectively. The more I did kiirtan, the more my internal clashes dissolved and the more connected I felt to my deepest Inner Self, and my life's work came into focus as my spirituality developed. I also witnessed others doing kiirtan and was deeply moved by its transformative powers, how it could: put people into a state of samadhi or 'absolute absorption into the divine'; heal grief, depression, anxiety, and various mental complexes; improve vocal abilities and inspire incredible new ideas, give protection against natural and man - made disasters; and most of all, bring one into closer proximity with the divine. During the years 1980- 1990 I visited my guru Shrii Shrii Anandamurti (affectionately known as Baba) in India as often as possible and sang kiirtan for Him on each occasion. It didn't seem to matter whether I was alone or in a group doing kiirtan, the intensity of love and devotion was all that really counted.

One day in my personal contact with Baba in 1979 in Jamaica, Baba asked me, what was my name and then said 'effulgence'. He also asked me what my duty was, I told Him Hari Parimandala Gosthi, (a department of Ananda Marga whose main service is kiirtan). Baba gave me a huge smile and pretended to play the guitar, teasing me in a loving way. He then touched my head and gave me His blessing. For the next two weeks I was in a state of absolute bliss, where everything inside and outside was full of effulgence. I will never forget Baba's pleasure as He imitated me playing kiirtan with my guitar. On another occasion while singing Kiirtan outside His house at Ananda Nagar, Baba said that one should use local instruments. In this way I understood that Kiirtan is not only to be played with Indian instruments but local western instruments as well including the guitar. Another time Baba said "perfect tune, perfect melody" about my kiirtan to Didi Ananda Tapasiddha who told me this many years later. At Ananda Nagar in the 80's, Baba also gave my guitar a name, Madhu Madhu, meaning 'sweet, sweet'. Hence, this with this constant support from my guru in kiirtan I had no doubt that this was to be my path, with my guitar providing the perfect companion. One of the greatest joys of my life was being able to experience kiirtan in Baba's blissful presence, to experience the devotion it arouses, and the sweet collective flow.

After Shrii Shrii Anandamurti left His body I studied ethnomusicology and through various incidents was lead to research the ancient kiirtan tradition of Rárh, India. This research continues till the present day, with my latest project being the Rárhi Kiirtan Competition and Festival that is held each year, organised by my research partner Sanjay (Tinku) Mahato of Dabar village and me. This Competition/Festival is a way of giving back to the tradition that has nourished me and countless other kiirtaniyas (kiirtan players) over the centuries, to honour and celebrate this tradition. Village kiirtan teams come from near and far to participate as well as the audience. More information can be found on Rárhi Marai Kiirtan Competition/ Festival on my website and Facebook.

INTRODUCTION

What is Kiirtan?

Kiirtan come from 'kiirt' in Sanskrit and means 'loud'. Kiirtan is one of the oldest forms of music in the world as one can imagine people in ancient times calling to their goddess/god for rain, for protection, in celebration, etc. and they would undoubtedly call and sing very loudly. Whether it was around the fire under the moonlight or during the day under the hot sun, kiirtan had a place in everyone's life, young and old, as it does today. Kiirtan has been through many transformations, permutations and developments since then and has always held a very significant place in our lives, as we call and sing to the Beloved.

The Three Styles of Kiirtan

There are three styles of kiirtan, each of which are equally significant. Firstly, there is pada, kiirtan, pada means 'verse' in Sanskrit. Pada kiirtans are praise songs, descriptive of the divine and Her/His qualities. There is a rich literary tradition of pada or kiiirtan songs in both the east and west. In the ancient land of Rárh (north east India) for example, there are Radha/Krishna kiirtans of Jayadeva (Giitagovinda), Candidasa, Narrottama Dasa, Govinda Das and many others, who composed kiirtans from the 11th century onwards. The second style of kiirtan is nama kirtan, or 'calling and chanting the name of the divine only', invented by Caitanya Mahaprabhu in the 15th century. Many of the popular kiirtans (hymns) in the west are of both pada and nama kiirtan, including Bach and Handel's Hallelujah chorus for example. Most of the kiirtans in this book start as a pada or kiirtan song and end in a nama kiirtan, as is traditional. The third kiirtan style is called Katha kiirtan 'stories' or narratives, put to music. These narratives are on the lives of Shiva and Parvati, Krishna and Radha, Jesus and other deities or saintly beings.

The Kiirtan of Rárh

The transformational experience of hearing a Rárhi Kiirtan group (Rárh is an Austric word, meaning 'red' as in red soil, and is in north east India), for the first time on a fieldwork trip in India in 2000 changed my perception of kiirtan forever. The supra aesthetic science of kiirtan (Prabhat Ranjan Sarkar, 1987) was only made apparent to me at this time. From that moment I knew I had to delve deep down into the science of kiirtan and discover the musical mechanics behind its supra 'transcendental' effect. I was lead down a very deep valley and into the musical goldmine of Rárh where the marai 'circular' kiirtan of in the villages was being done especially in the summer season. As part of my PhD (SOAS, London University) I documented   the kiirtan tradition in Rárh over the period 2005-10 and still continue today. However, it was only after my viva in 2010 that I really began to put the pieces of the puzzle together, and see the larger picture, as to how kiirtan's supra aesthetic science actually works. And so it continues to be a mission of mine to unravel the depth and beauty of kiirtan and to share the knowledge and the ecstatic devotion that it arouses, through supporting the annual Competition/Festival in Rárh and in kiirtan workshops worldwide.

---

[1] Prabhat Ranjan Sarkar, 1987, Samgiita, Ananda Marga Publications, India.

The Purpose of this Kiirtan Book

In an Indian context, kiirtan is samgiita, i.e., song, dance and instrumental music. As guitar is an important accompanying instrument in kiirtan, it thus fits within the category of samgiita. The purpose behind this first kiirtan book is to present some new and old Baba Nam Kevalam kiirtans as a resource for kiirtan players/singers and to promote kiirtan as a genre in itself, much like jazz or classical music, with its own composers, and compositions, which are still relatively unknown and so broaden the therefore knowledge and repertoire of kiirtan itself. So, each of the kiirtans in this book have a story to it, which I have shared in some cases depending on space and will elaborate upon in future books to follow. Thank you for taking the time to read and to practice these kiirtans, all of which came about at pivotal points on my spiritual journey and provided me with a means to communicate directly with the divine. I now delight in sharing these with you.

The Guitar

The Guitar is a very beautiful and flexible instrument. Its size means that it can be held comfortably close to the body, and it can voice a multitude of emotions and dynamics through its melodic and percussive capabilities. That's why it is perfect for kiirtan, where all our emotions can be expressed and channelled towards the divine. Unlike some larger instruments, the guitar is portable and can be carried easily while dancing (lalita marmika). So as the guitar is primarily an accompanying instrument in kiirtan, like the harmonium, its primary function being to provide melodic and rhythmic support to the vocalist, who in turn works in collaboration with the drummers, cymbal players and other instrumentalists.

The Chords and Capo: Most of the chords in the book are open chords so as to provide an easy introduction to kiirtan. There's a multitude of guitar books in the market which provide a good introduction to guitar theory at a beginner's level. Depending on the key of the kiirtan, the capo should be placed on the fret that suits your voice. In future, it will be possible to change the key while playing kiirtan, without using a capo, but in the beginning it is necessary to have one.

Videos: Each kiirtan has an accompanying video on how to play it, which is available as part of the booklet. These videos can be downloaded from my website at www.Jyoshnamusic.com

Acknowledgements:

My gratitude goes to Kavita for her formatting skills; to Didi Ananda Prama for her love and hospitality; to Erik Azzopardi for his friendship and brilliant editing skills; and Jano Stefanik for his wonderful support in publishing this book, to Isabel Komalgiiti my little one, and those of you who have supported me all along.
Thankyou.
With Love, Jyoshna

You are Mine Kiirtan (aka My Golden Guru)

From *Touched by the Sea* album

You are mine and no one else's, You belong to me and nobody else
And I am Yours and no one else's, I belong to You and nobody else

1. When my days are full of shadow
I sit and call Your name out loud
And the core that lies within me
Rises above, my insecurity

2. When the pain's tearing my body
I offer it for you to see
You're the lover, that holds within me
Come and take it gently from me.

3. When the joy fountain springs upwards
Every drop, pure mystery
When it's touched by Your loving
Come, come rain, rain down upon me

Copyright ©1988 Jyoshna

'When We All Break Down' Kiirtan
From the *Dharmacakra* album

Singing songs of liberation
With people of different creeds and nations
Though our needs are the same, our fears, joys and pains
How can we all come together?
When we all break down
Our heads to the ground
Opening our hearts in sweet surrender
When we all break down
Our heads to the ground
Opening our hearts in sweet surrender
Baba Nam Kevalam (repeats)

Copyright Jyoshna © 2010

Travelling Dom Kiirtan aka Tantra Pith I

From *Sounds of Silence* album

Sitting beneath an ancient tree at Ananda Nagar, India in 1996, I saw in my meditation,
a group of travelling Dom musicians travelling along the pathway singing this melody.

Copyright © Jyoshna 1996

6

Devii Kiirtan

From *Sounds of Silence* album

Copyright © Jyoshna 1996

Tiny Green Island

8

me   The Great is with me   Ba - ba Nam Ke-va-lam Ba-ba, Ba - ba Nam Ke-va-
lam   Ba - ba Nam Ke-va-lam Ba-ba, Ba - ba Nam Ke-va - lam   Ba-ba Nam Ke-va-
lam   Ba-ba Nam Ke-va - lam   Ba-ba Nam Ke-va - lam   Ba-ba Nam Ke-va-
lam   Ba   ba Nam Ke-va - lam Ba-ba,   Ba - ba Nam Ke-va - lam   Ba
ba Nam Ke-va-lam Ba-ba Ba - ba Nam ke-va - lam   Ba-ba_ Nam Ke-va- lam   Ba-ba
Nam_ Ke - va - lam   Ba-ba Nam Ke-va - lam   Ba-ba Nam_ Ke - va - lam
Ba - ba Nam_   Ke - va - lam   Ba - ba Nam_   Ke - va - lam
Ba-ba Nam Ke - va - lam   Ba - ba Nam Ke - va - lam

Irish Traveller Kiirtan

From *Avarta Kiirtan* album

Copyright © Jyoshna 2016

11

Victory Kiirtan Chorus

Theobald House Kiirtan

Jyoshna

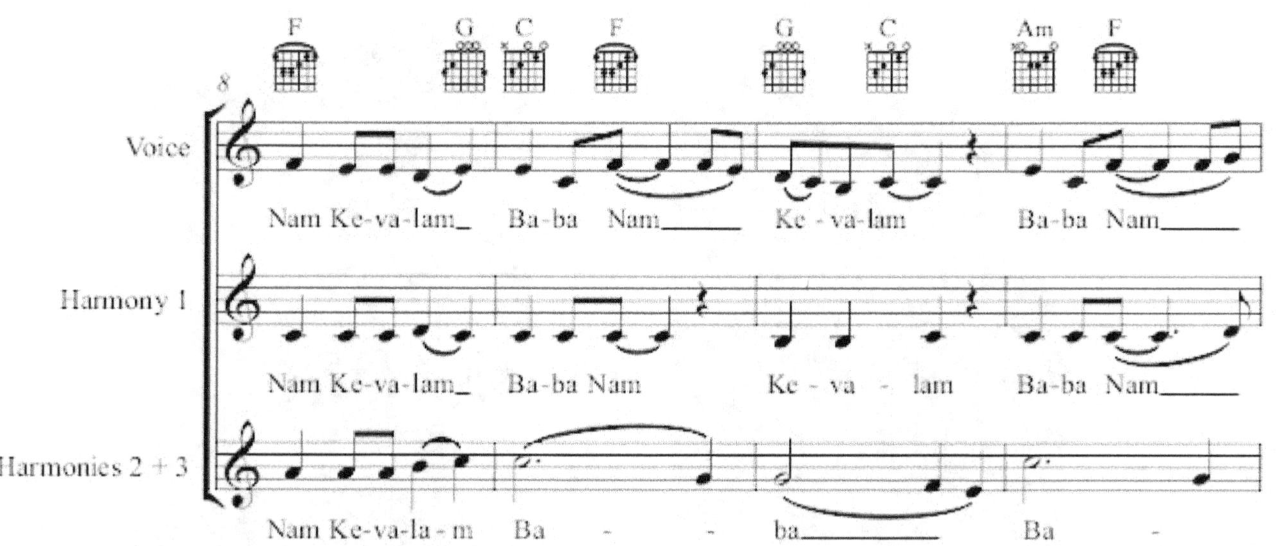

Copyright © Jyoshna 2005

12

This kiirtan was composed while living in Theobalds House, in London. We would start our days with kirtan at 5 am each morning and this would give us tremendous energy and inspiration for the day. I had just started a PhD at SOAS on Music and was researching everything related to Rarhi Kiirtan. I would especially like to thank Karun Towsey for his generous hospitality and culinary skills.

Ananda Sutram Kirtan 1
from *'Dharmacakra'* album

Jyoshna

This kiirtan is inspired by Shrii Shrii Anandamurti's Ananda Sutram Chapter I:
The Brahmacakra (Cycle of Creation)

no 1:7 Drk Purusah Dharshanam Shaktishca
Purusha is the ultimate witness and Prakriti is the 'act of witnessing' and 'that which is witnessed'
no 1:8 Gunabandanena Gunabhivyakti
As the gunas 'binding factors' increase their bondage, they express themselves fully in the emergence of the fundamental factors of the creation cycle.

Copyright © Jyoshna 2016

Children's Kirtan March

From *Live in Brazil* album

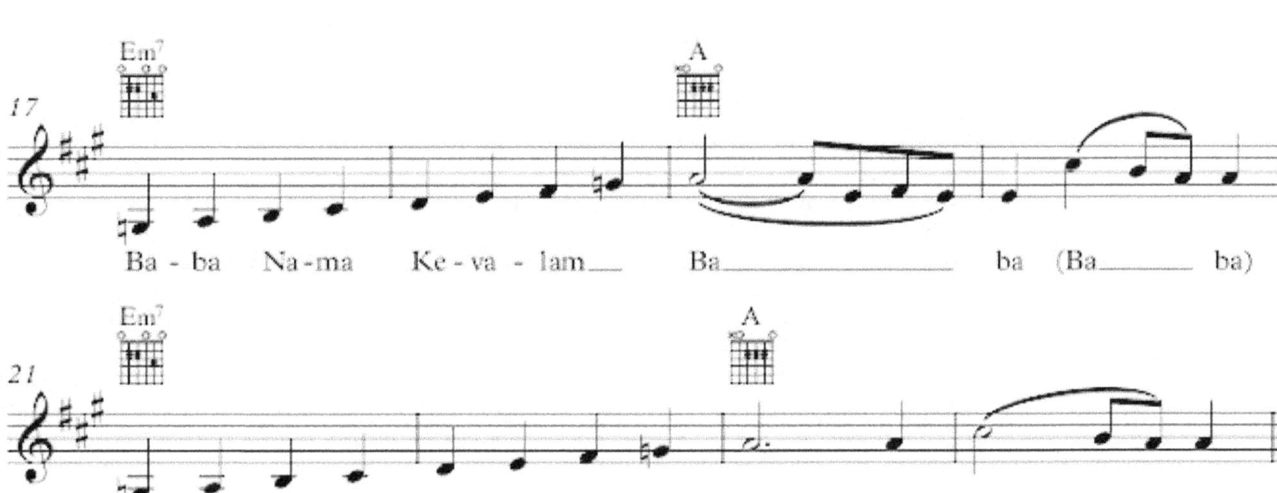

Copyright © Jyoshna 2008

Lily and the Moon Kiirtan

from *Touched by the Sea* album

Jyoshna

Open my eyes, I look at You
I see myself, melt to a pool
What can I say? What can I do?
You pull on strings I can't undo.
And I'm thinking of You, thinking of You

2. Just like a lily in muddy pond
She fights all day and all night long
Amidst storms and pouring rain
Her existance eeked out among the pain
And it's only the moonlight, it's only the moonlight
That keeps her strong, to carry on
Thinking of One,
Baba Nam Kevalam, Baba Nam Kevalam x 2

3. Tantrikas take up the fight, against wrongs with all your might
A pauseless struggle cannot cease
Until we have equality,
And it's only the moonlight, it's only the moonlight
That keeps her strong, to carry on,
Thinking of One
Baba Nam Kevalam, repeats.

Copyright © Jyoshna 1993

Clarion Call Kiirtan

Copyright © Jyoshna 2018

18

For Grace Kiirtan (aka If Not For You)

From the *Avarta Kiirtan* album

This kiirtan is dedicated to Grace, Didi Ananda Prama's beloved dog, who was living on Sunrise Farm for many years. Unfortunately when Didi was in Haiti, doing relief work Grace became ill. At the same time, this kiirtan tune kept coming into my mind when I woke. So we sang it to Grace as she left this world.

Verse 1. If not for You, the flowers in my garden they would never bloom
The birds high in the trees would never sing a tune
The sun way in the sky would never touch the moon
2. You and I, nothing in this world could make me say goodbye
Heaven on the earth would only cry
Without you, everything would simply disappear
Bridge: I just want you to know that even though I'm afraid
Lacking confidence most of the day
But I would do anything and everything for You
Till the day I die I realise, that only this is true
3. With your touch every particle is filled with love
every thing below is, as above,
Spiralling above the fire, white turtle doves
4. Finally the moment has arrived
In your arms I know love will never die
Everything inside my heart has come alive

Copyright © Jyoshna 2016

Kiirtan Chord Chart

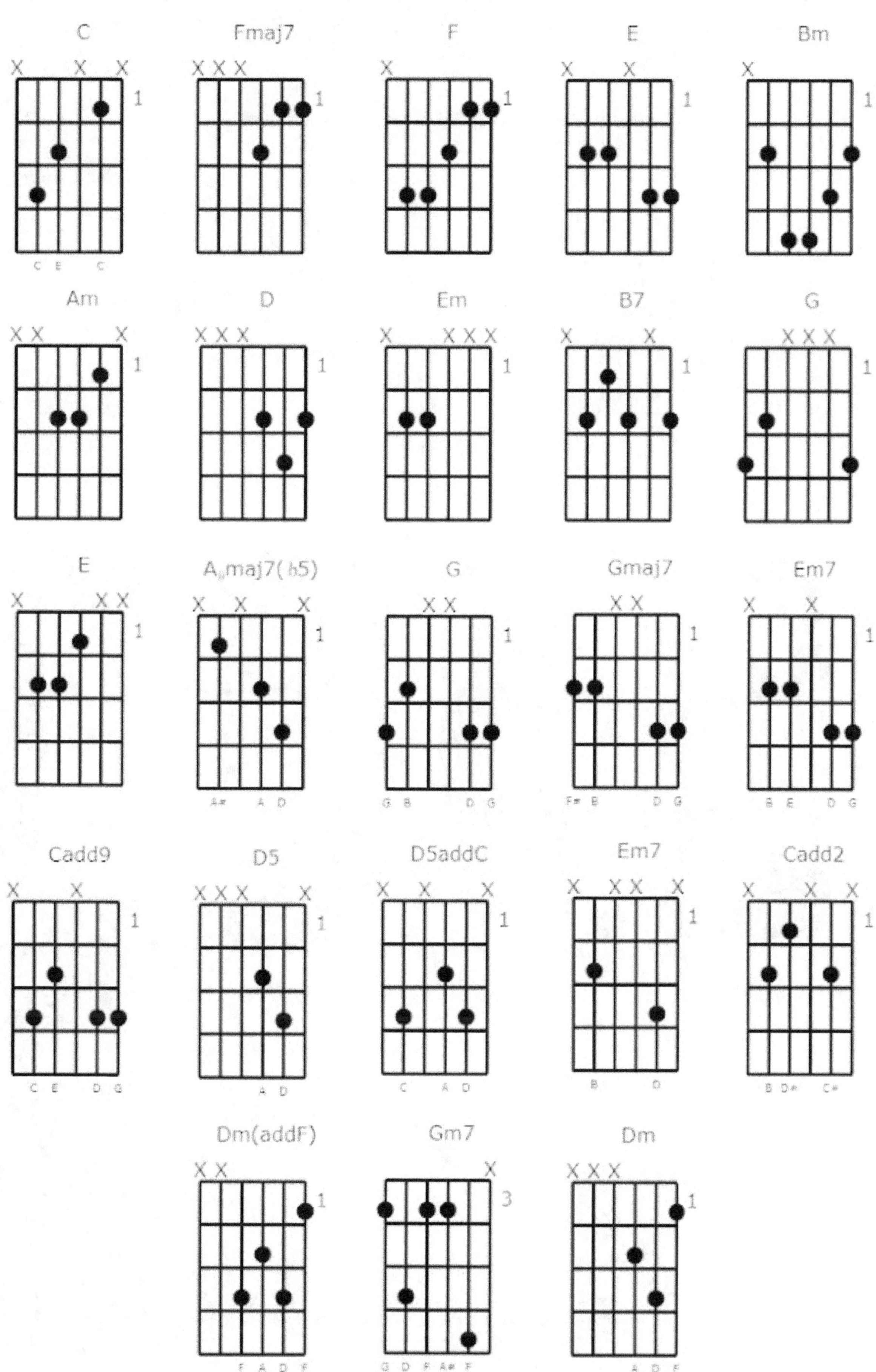

The kiirtans that feature in this booklet come from the albums below:
Touched by The Sea, Sound of Silence, Live in Brazil, Dharma Cakra, Avarta Kirtan

They are available at www.jyoshnamusic.com

imeo Links for Kiirtan Guitar Videos by Jyoshna:

1. You are Mine Kiirtan – Password: Kiirtan Guitar 1
https://vimeo.com/284477859

2. "When we all break down" kiirtan – Password: Kiirtan Guitar 2
https://vimeo.com/285797917

3. Travelling Dom Kiirtan – Password : Kiirtan Guitar 3
https://vimeo.com/281705490

4. Devii Kiirtan – Password : Kiirtan Guitar 4
https://vimeo.com/284387661

4. Devii Kiirtan Chords – Password : Kiirtan Guitar 4A
https://vimeo.com/284393557

5. Tiny Green Island Song – Password: Kiirtan Guitar 5
https://vimeo.com/284394464

5. Tiny Green Island Kiirtan – Password: Kiirtan Guitar 5A
https://vimeo.com/284396484

6. The Irish Travellers Kiirtan – Password: Kiirtan Guitar 6
https://vimeo.com/284433540

7. Victory Kiirtan – Password: Kiirtan Guitar 7
https://vimeo.com/284434644

8. Ananda Sutram Kiirtan – Password: Kiirtan Guitar 8
https://vimeo.com/285798976

9. Childrens Kiirtan March Kiirtan – Password: Kiirtan Guitar 9
https://vimeo.com/285800823

10. Lily and the Moon – Password: Kiirtan Guitar 10
https://vimeo.com/284436635

11. Clarion Call Kiirtan – Password: Kiirtan Guitar 11
https://vimeo.com/285802037

12. For Grace Kiirtan – Password: Kiirtan Guitar 12
https://vimeo.com/285806073

Kiirtan **Guitar**

1. *You Are Mine Kiirtan*
2. *We All Break Down Kiirtan*
3. *Travelling Dom Kiirtan*
4. *Devii Kiirtan*
5. *Tiny Green Island Kiirtan*
6. *Irish Traveller Kiirtan*
7. *Victory Kiirtan*
8. *Ananda Sutram Kiirtan*
9. *Children's Kiirtan March*
10. *Lily and The Moon Kiirtan*
11. *Clarion Call Kiirtan*
12. *For Grace Kiirtan*

All the sound files can be downloaded at www.jyoshnamusic.com

Sunrise Farm, Derryouran, Whitegate, Co. Clare, V94HY96, Ireland.

Copyright © Jyoshna 2018

www.ingramcontent.com/pod-product-compliance
Lightning Source LLC
Chambersburg PA
CBHW080251180726
47999CB00019B/2835